GOLDEN RECORD

ROSEMARY VALERO-O'CONNELL

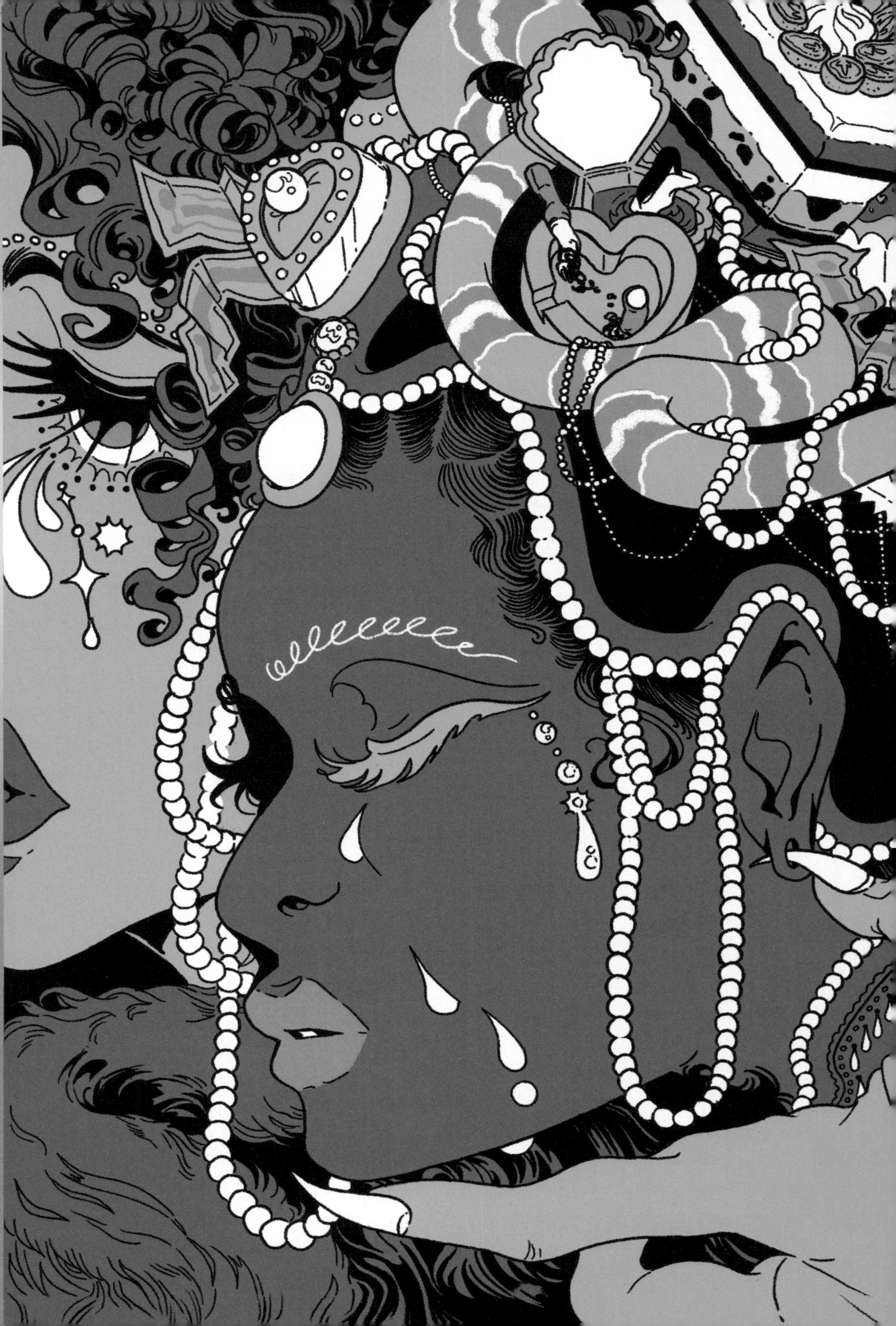

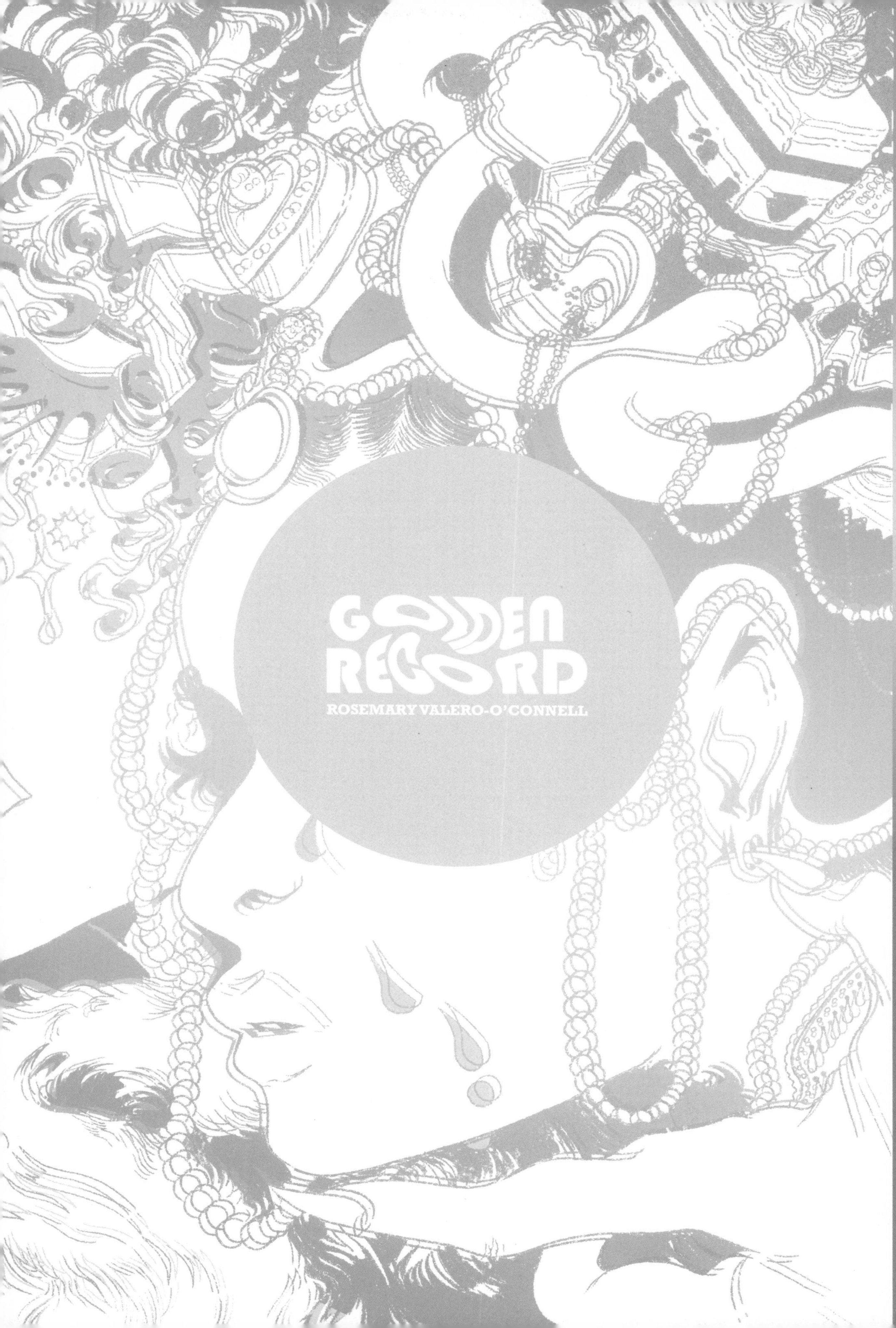
GOLDEN RECORD
ROSEMARY VALERO-O'CONNELL

aperitivo

cuerpo como beast to be bled, como scorched
leather, como tallow on the butcher's floor.
an old friend you can't look in the eye.

plato fuerte

cuerpo como locked door, como bloodless host,
como ripened pericarp.
a thick velvet curtain sieving out moonlight.

aguardiente

cuerpo como radiant bridge, como first bloom,
como beginning and end.
the rock you turn over in your garden to find me.

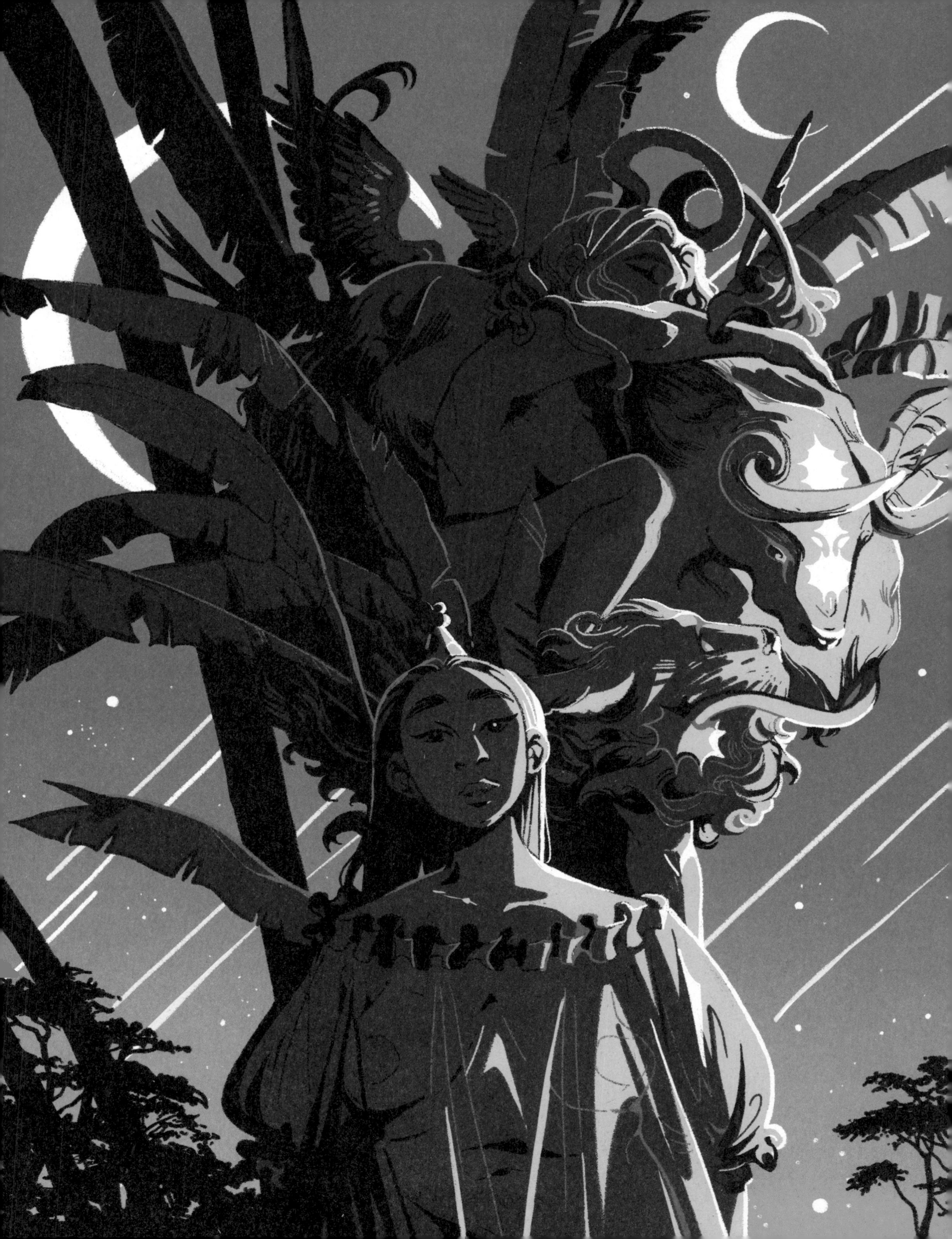

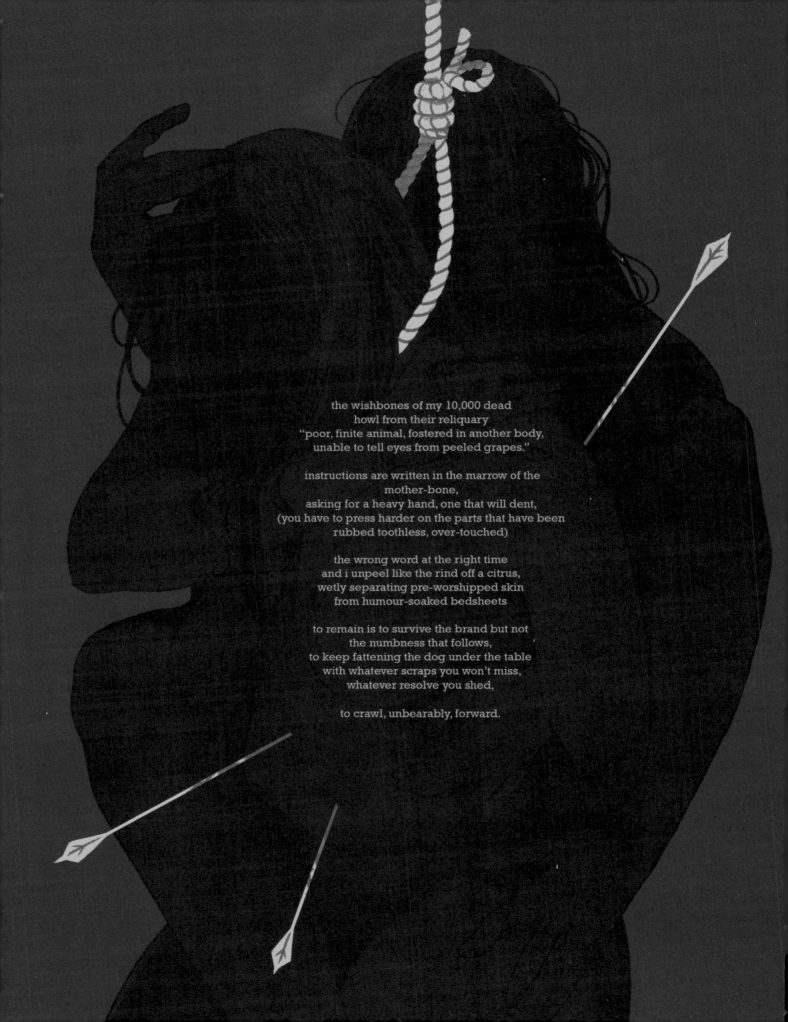

the wishbones of my 10,000 dead
howl from their reliquary
"poor, finite animal, fostered in another body,
unable to tell eyes from peeled grapes."

instructions are written in the marrow of the
mother-bone,
asking for a heavy hand, one that will dent,
(you have to press harder on the parts that have been
rubbed toothless, over-touched)

the wrong word at the right time
and i unpeel like the rind off a citrus,
wetly separating pre-worshipped skin
from humour-soaked bedsheets

to remain is to survive the brand but not
the numbness that follows,
to keep fattening the dog under the table
with whatever scraps you won't miss,
whatever resolve you shed,

to crawl, unbearably, forward.

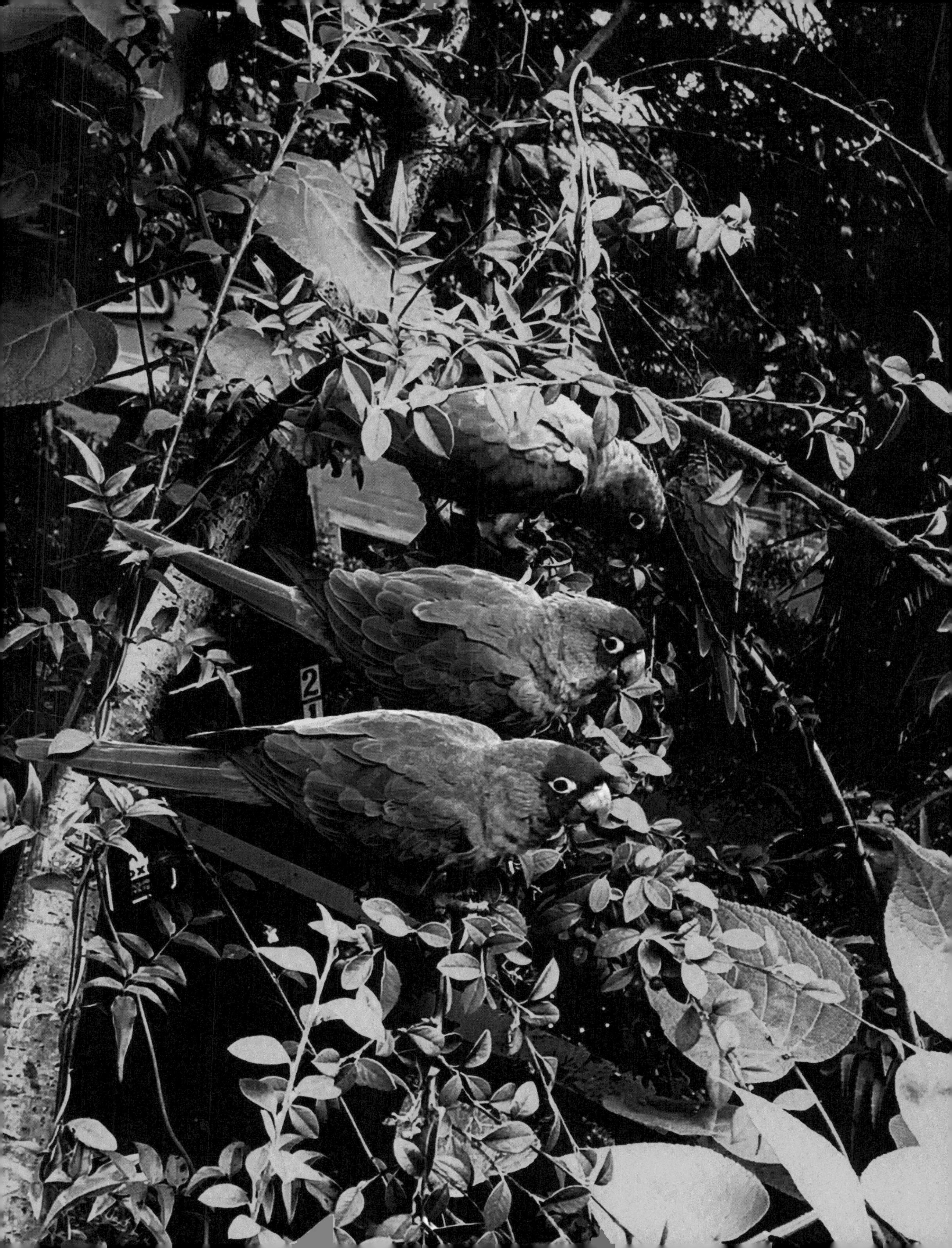

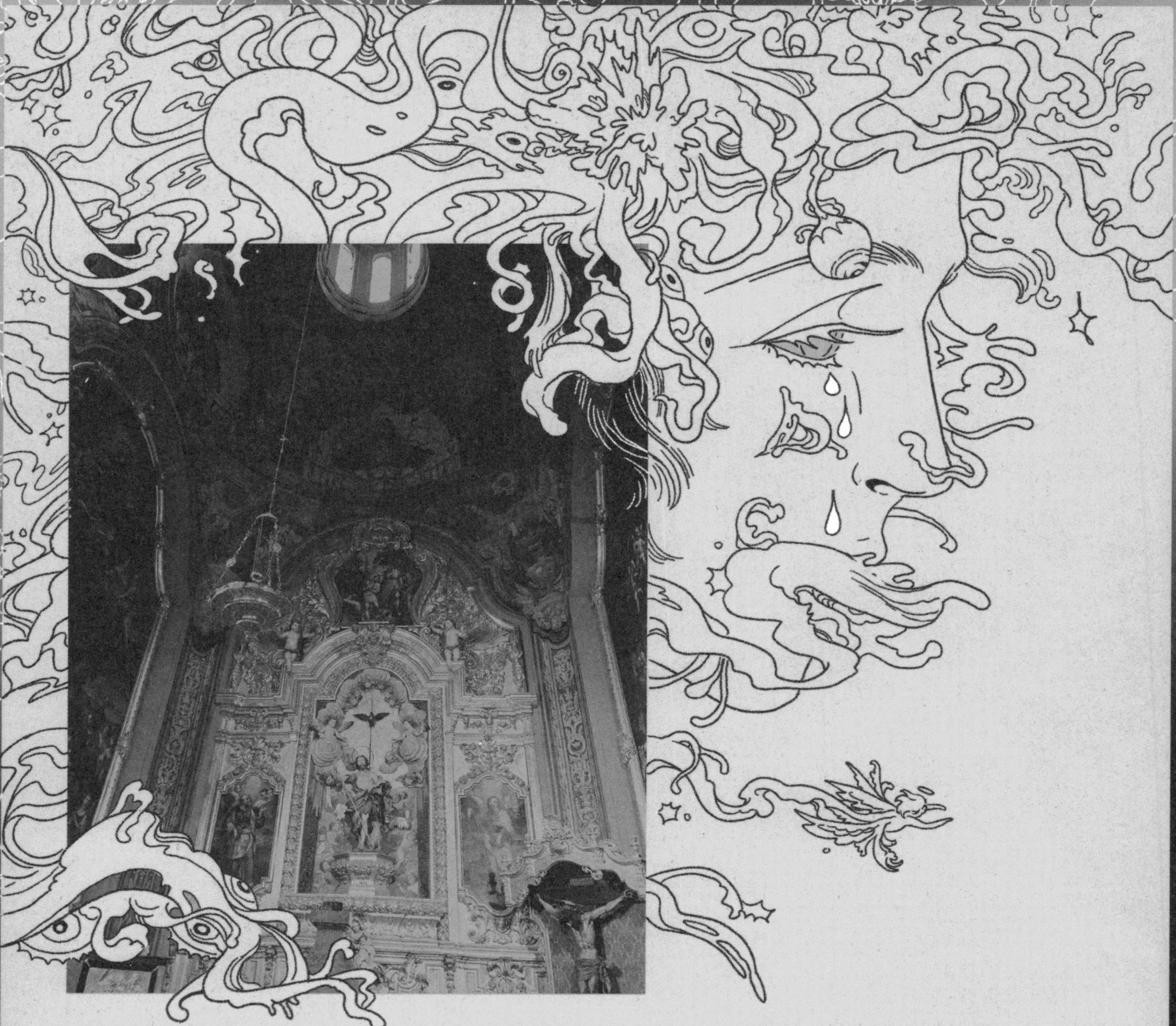

the space between my mouth and your shoulder crackles like
struck quartz, haloed in wet lipgloss, in iris heart notes,
pink neon blushing on the bar's cheekbones.
our thighs stick, bread filling under heat,
angel butter, swan down.
in a house, in a room, in a bed, in the palm of your hand.

your hair on my pillow, like meat bursting from a cracked crab
leg, like egg yolk dropped in howling water, like one hundred
other meals i had before arriving at your table.
paradise is a dripping greenhouse at the bottom of the earth
where you can pull me like a pearl from the mouth of an oyster,
feel the snap of my pink connective tissue,
dress me in plastic flowers and bring me down from the
mountain.

i want to be champagne and sambac jasmine to you,
instead i will be the worst thing you ever do to him.

you'll tell me, twice bitten calf, body angled
against mine so your breathing heats my
heart like bellows, how easily it could have
been me.

some moments are fastened to me como un
muñeco del día de los inocentes, pinned to
the back of my eyelids with a lepidopterist's
learned touch.

halved pomegranate, unclean cut,
we have no exits left to take.

palms warm with oil,
the massage therapist will dip her hands
into the cup of your bones
and pull up the stone of pain
          (smooth, perfect)
that's made its home under your wings,
pinfeathers growing through
cracks in the china,
remnants of the night she couldn't help
but break every bone in the house.

gutted fish on her table
in upturned supplication,
you'll think, how obvious,
que poca originalidad tiene el cuerpo,
but your body is the only atlas
she gave you to her burning,
so you swallow the stone back down
and wait for wisdom.

en la cuna del incendio, clean the weak
watercolor of her shadow off the floors
of a place that battered you both,
try to feel for doves under her skin.
the halls sag with the salt
of her sea changes, gelatin marrying
the hardwood as she soaks
through the floorboards
so slowly you almost let her.

every corner breeds the young of ghosts,
formless under the rotoscope,
mouthfuls of charred film you can't
taste around.

when you could get close enough to touch,
to hold, you'd think,
     (finally a use for this drooling clay body,
  to ground the lightning that comes off of you
               hold all that wailing electricity
                    against my soft palette)
you'd think,
     (the fruit is lucky not to feel itself rotting)

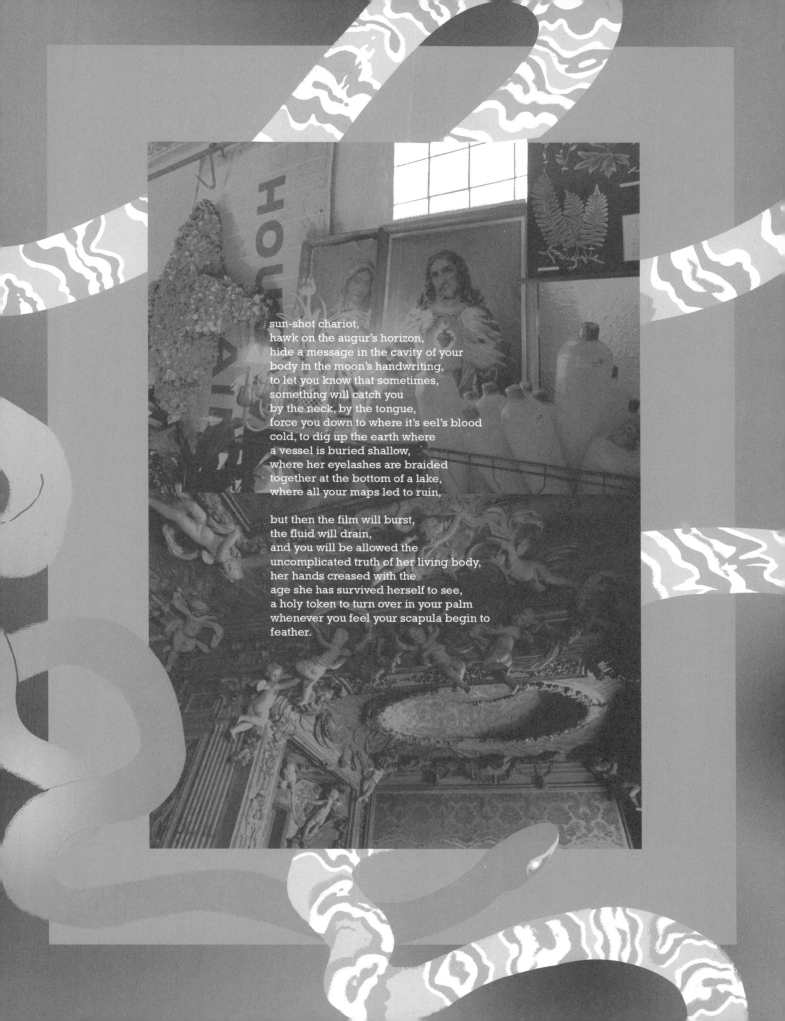

sun-shot chariot,
hawk on the augur's horizon,
hide a message in the cavity of your
body in the moon's handwriting,
to let you know that sometimes,
something will catch you
by the neck, by the tongue,
force you down to where it's eel's blood
cold, to dig up the earth where
a vessel is buried shallow,
where her eyelashes are braided
together at the bottom of a lake,
where all your maps led to ruin,

but then the film will burst,
the fluid will drain,
and you will be allowed the
uncomplicated truth of her living body,
her hands creased with the
age she has survived herself to see,
a holy token to turn over in your palm
whenever you feel your scapula begin to
feather.

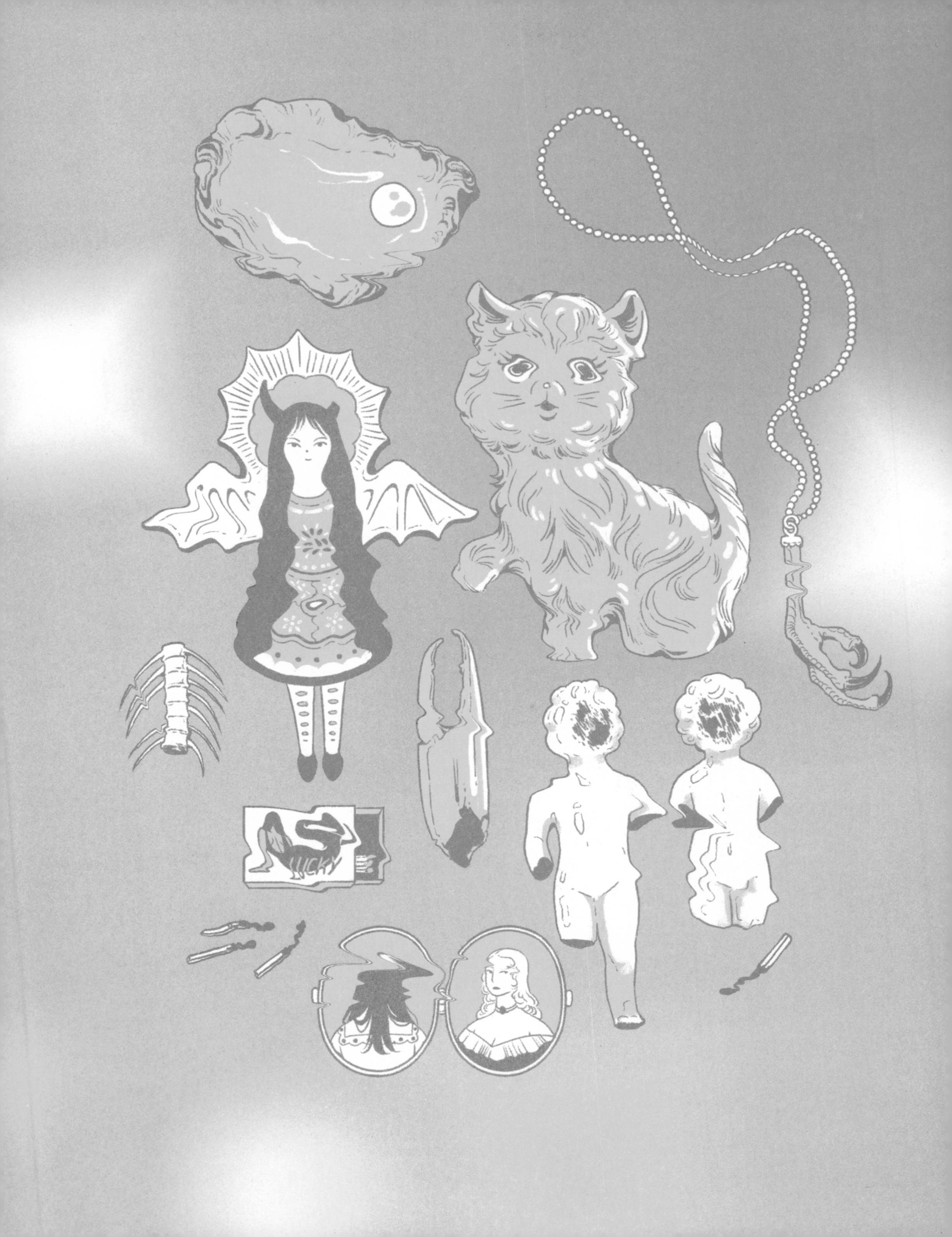
LUCKY

santísima, in ermine and lily,
give me something i can use,
that'll stick to my ribs,
so i won't digest my teeth in my mouth
rather than fill a room too well.

dame consuelo,
blinded, cooked in brandy,
and eaten whole in the deep dark,
come to me glazed in music
and warm sugar,
bedded in hazelnut and root vegetable,
in mushrooms taken from the garden
of a corpse.

sleep inside the dog that bites you
every morning, punish the overflow,
ignore the unshakeable pine and build
your house from wax and bile,
meet your collapse spitting vinegar,
writhing on the tile.

there is no price, no tithe,
only the indifferent dawn.
only the hands that picked the peach
and the eyes that watched the clouds boil,
the pulse in each bowl, the residue of the
work it takes to feed something,
lacquer over the part of you
that doesn't want to die empty.

resolution, sworn on the only thing i own:
i will grow lined inside my own heaving palace,
i will let my mouth hang slick with comb honey,
i won't gnaw the bit as i wax and wane.
i will let the one at the end of my throat climb my eyestalks like a wish unmade,
take the reins, her birthright,
and hope i am born in armor from her cleaved head,
i will braid her hair with my skeleton's hands as she starts us
on the long walk home.

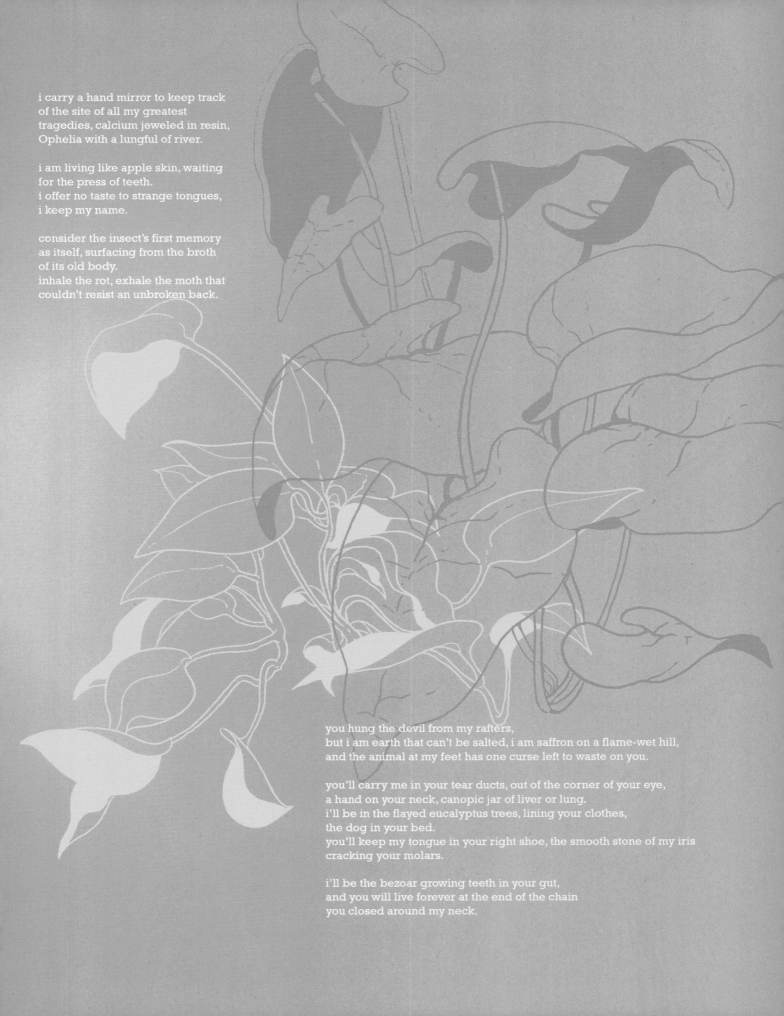

i carry a hand mirror to keep track
of the site of all my greatest
tragedies, calcium jeweled in resin,
Ophelia with a lungful of river.

i am living like apple skin, waiting
for the press of teeth.
i offer no taste to strange tongues,
i keep my name.

consider the insect's first memory
as itself, surfacing from the broth
of its old body.
inhale the rot, exhale the moth that
couldn't resist an unbroken back.

you hung the devil from my rafters,
but i am earth that can't be salted, i am saffron on a flame-wet hill,
and the animal at my feet has one curse left to waste on you.

you'll carry me in your tear ducts, out of the corner of your eye,
a hand on your neck, canopic jar of liver or lung.
i'll be in the flayed eucalyptus trees, lining your clothes,
the dog in your bed.
you'll keep my tongue in your right shoe, the smooth stone of my iris
cracking your molars.

i'll be the bezoar growing teeth in your gut,
and you will live forever at the end of the chain
you closed around my neck.

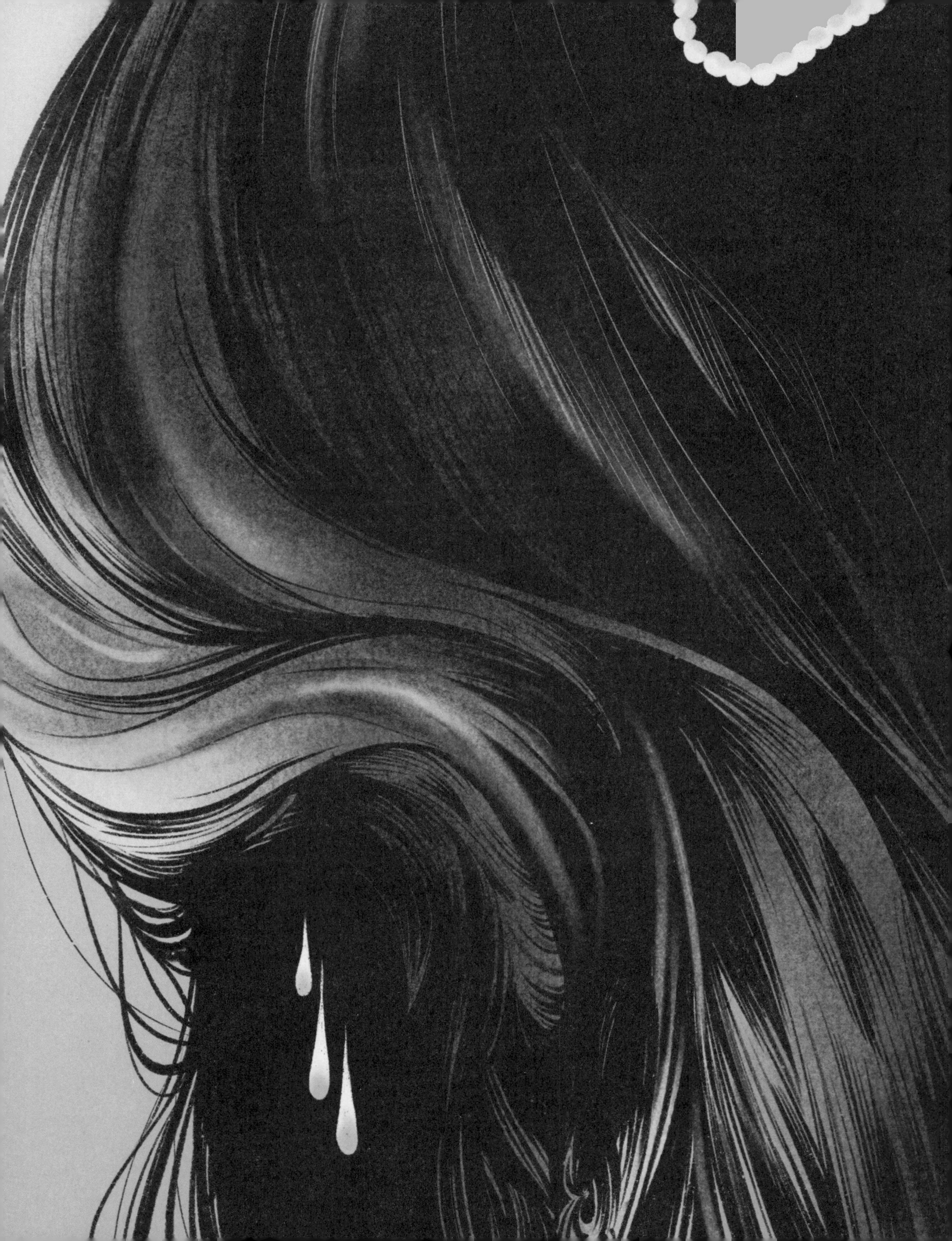

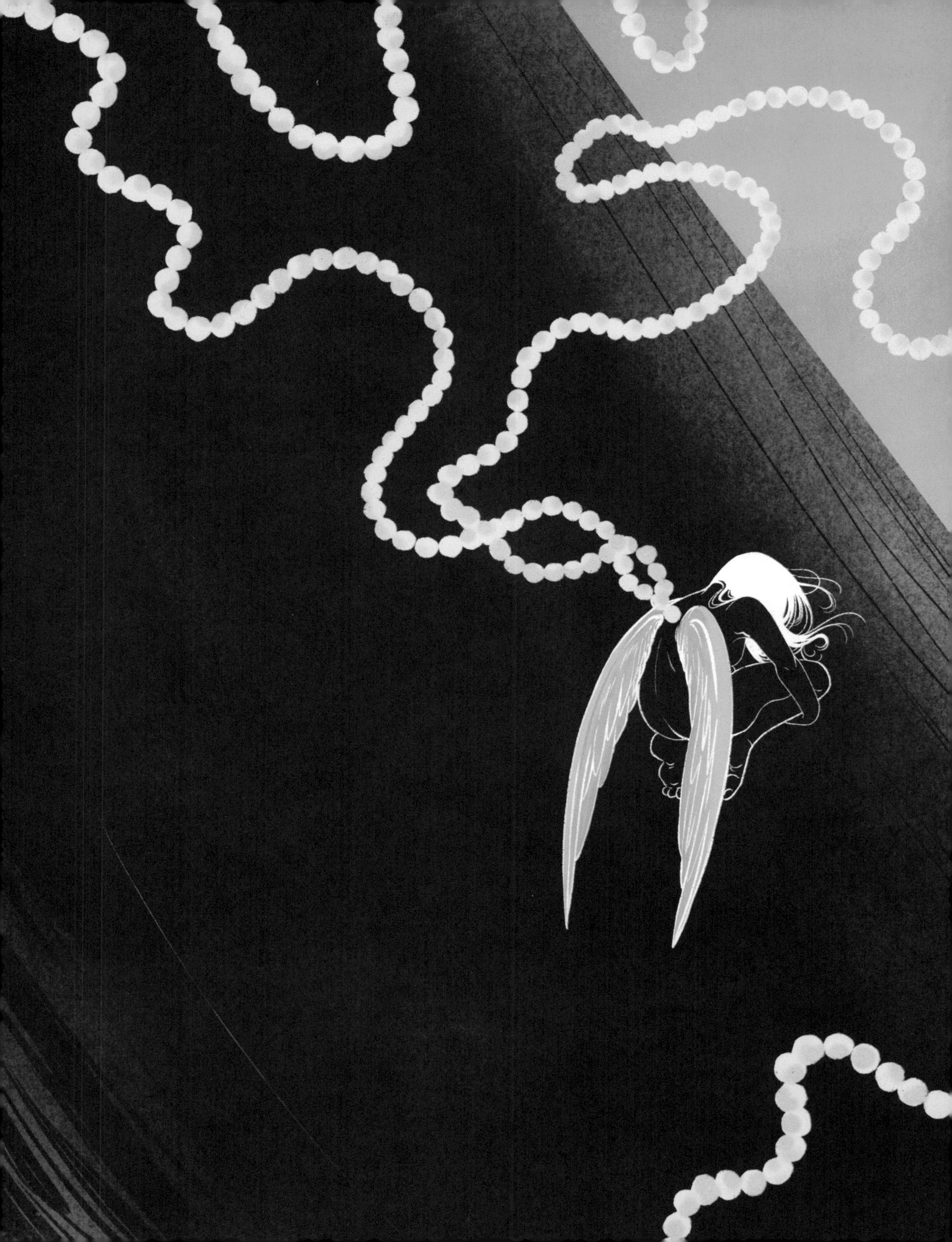

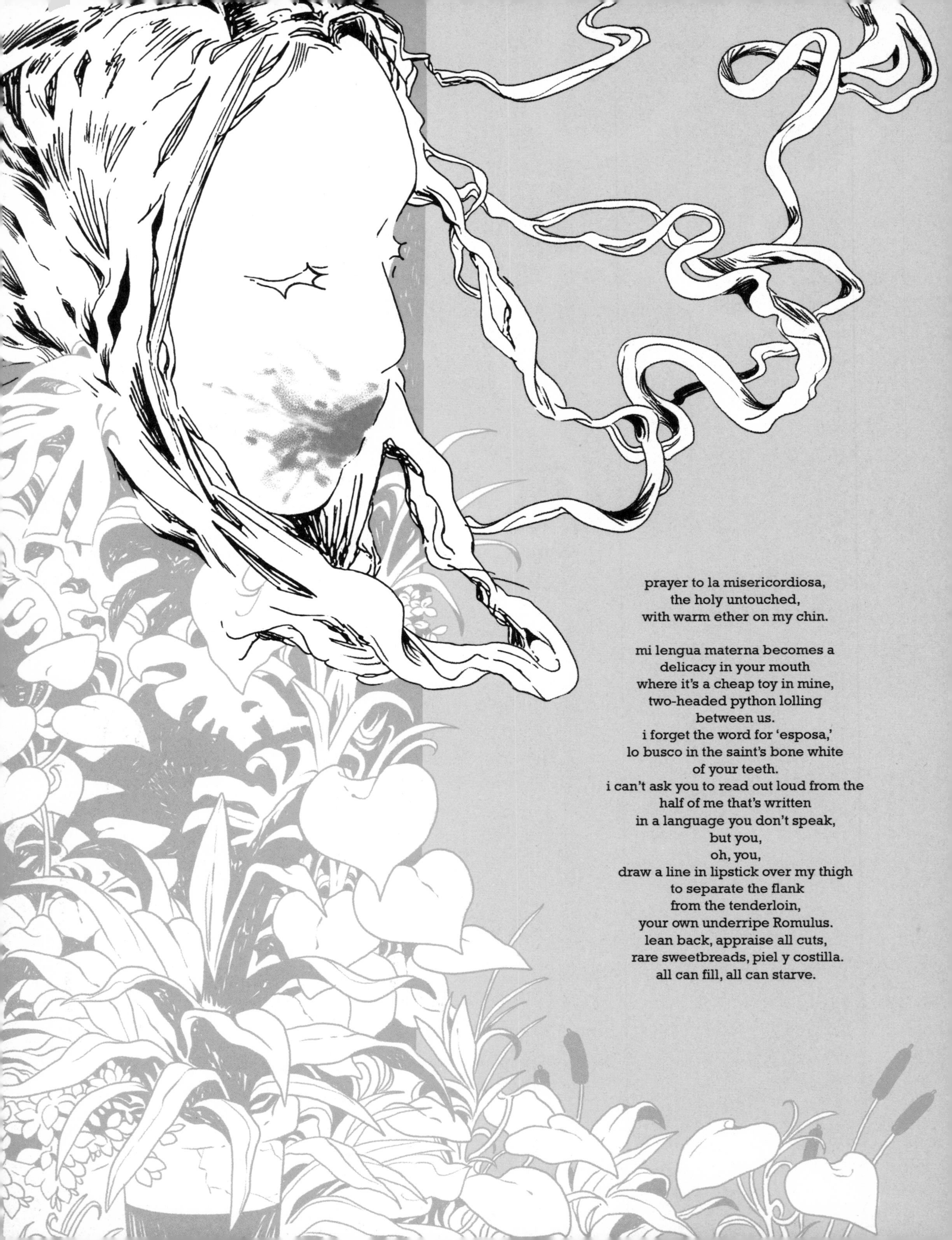

prayer to la misericordiosa,
the holy untouched,
with warm ether on my chin.

mi lengua materna becomes a
delicacy in your mouth
where it's a cheap toy in mine,
two-headed python lolling
between us.
i forget the word for 'esposa,'
lo busco in the saint's bone white
of your teeth.
i can't ask you to read out loud from the
half of me that's written
in a language you don't speak,
but you,
oh, you,
draw a line in lipstick over my thigh
to separate the flank
from the tenderloin,
your own underripe Romulus.
lean back, appraise all cuts,
rare sweetbreads, piel y costilla.
all can fill, all can starve.

your laughter heats the dusk,
and it shows me a door in my heart i'd never noticed before.

i put down roots in the curve of your back and there i'll remain,
lapping dew from cold china, harvesting the eggs left by the moon,
watering the persimmon trees with my spit 'til they grow.

ruined, thankfully

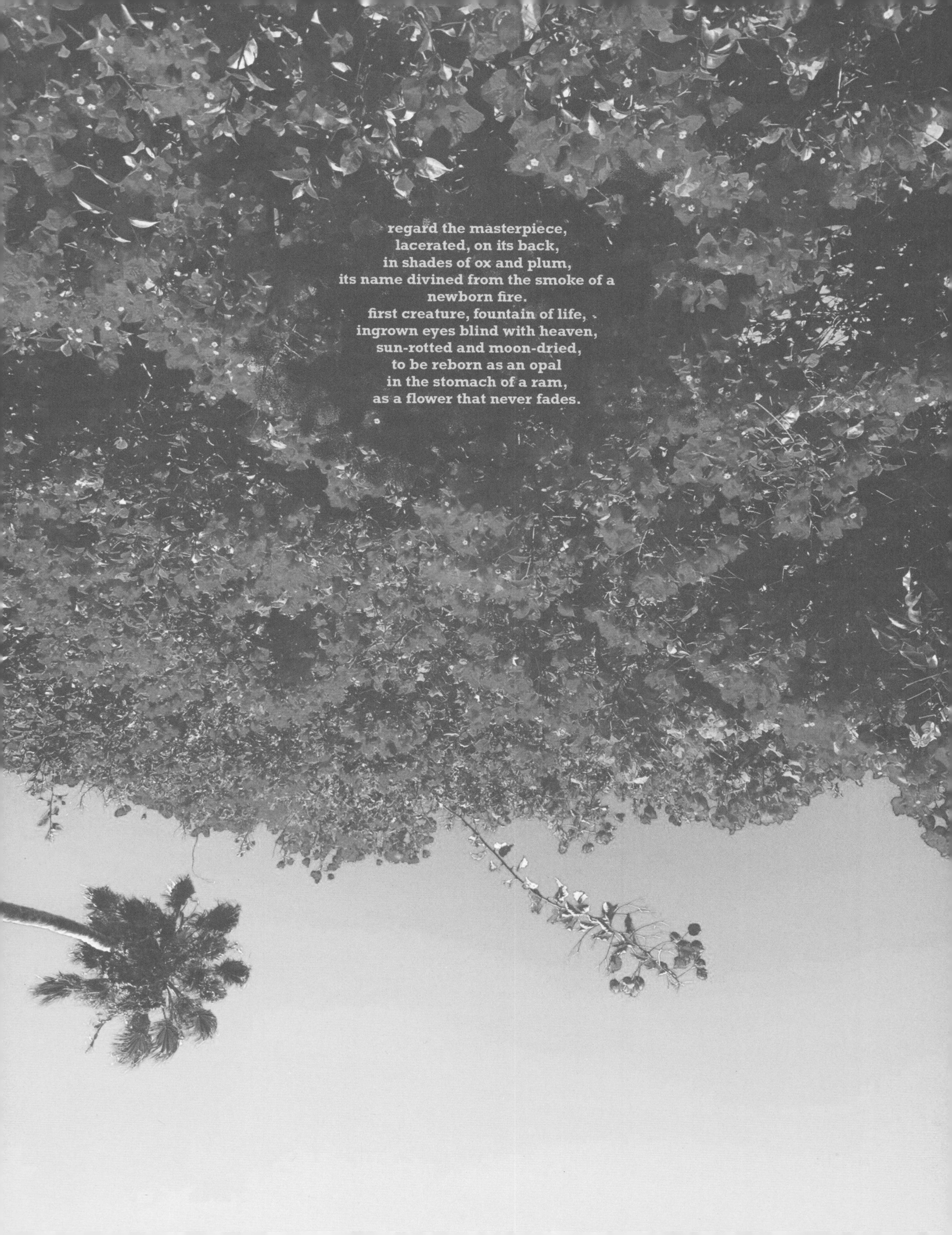

regard the masterpiece,
lacerated, on its back,
in shades of ox and plum,
its name divined from the smoke of a
newborn fire.
first creature, fountain of life,
ingrown eyes blind with heaven,
sun-rotted and moon-dried,
to be reborn as an opal
in the stomach of a ram,
as a flower that never fades.

XV

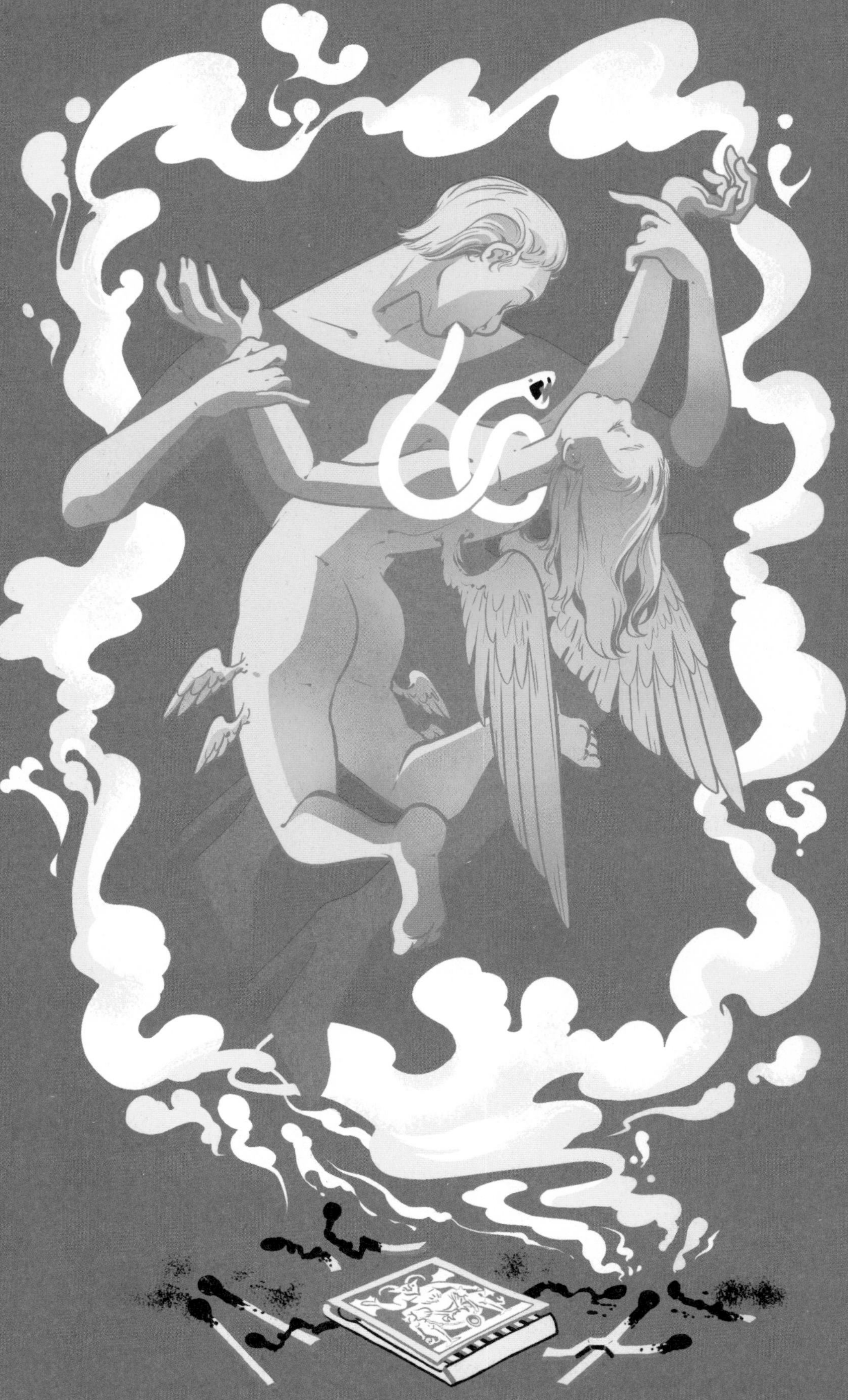

el diablo

it's like home, isn't it?

like beef, like pork, like venison,
like laughter, like ache, like heat,
like red rock vivisected,
like paprika on grilled skin,
like lace asleep in the grave,
like lacquered nails in opera gloves,
like aftershave and gasoline,
like footsteps in the salt cellar,
like a hurricane of swallows
shattering the dusk,
like incense and mascara,
like the hand inside the shadow
puppet, like purple rice and sea
grapes and broth made from your
grandmother's ashes,
like horseflies in an open wound,
like lichen on a statue's thigh,
like the painted wood of the cross,
like spit in the wrong throat,
like an axe through a bloodline,
like wine-stained teeth,
like valencia oranges, like snails
cooked in oil, like lanterns in the
distance,
like the only thing left of me is you,
like light and color and vomit,
like sheep's teeth wailing from the
bottom of the riverbed
after the rain

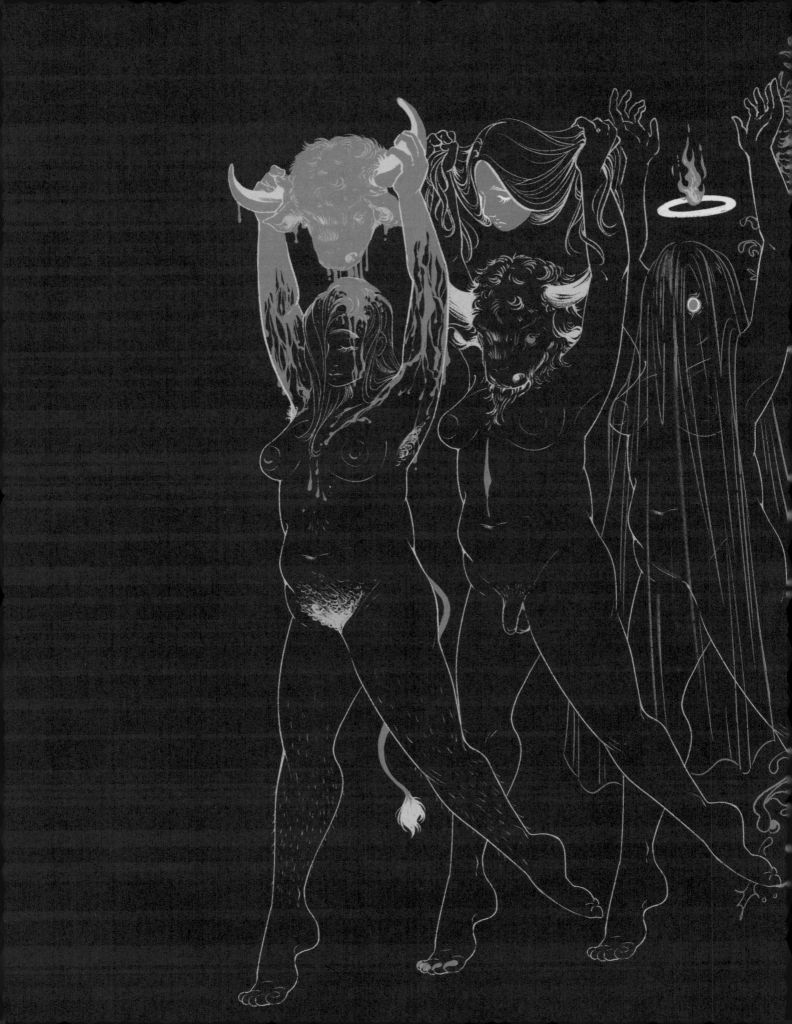

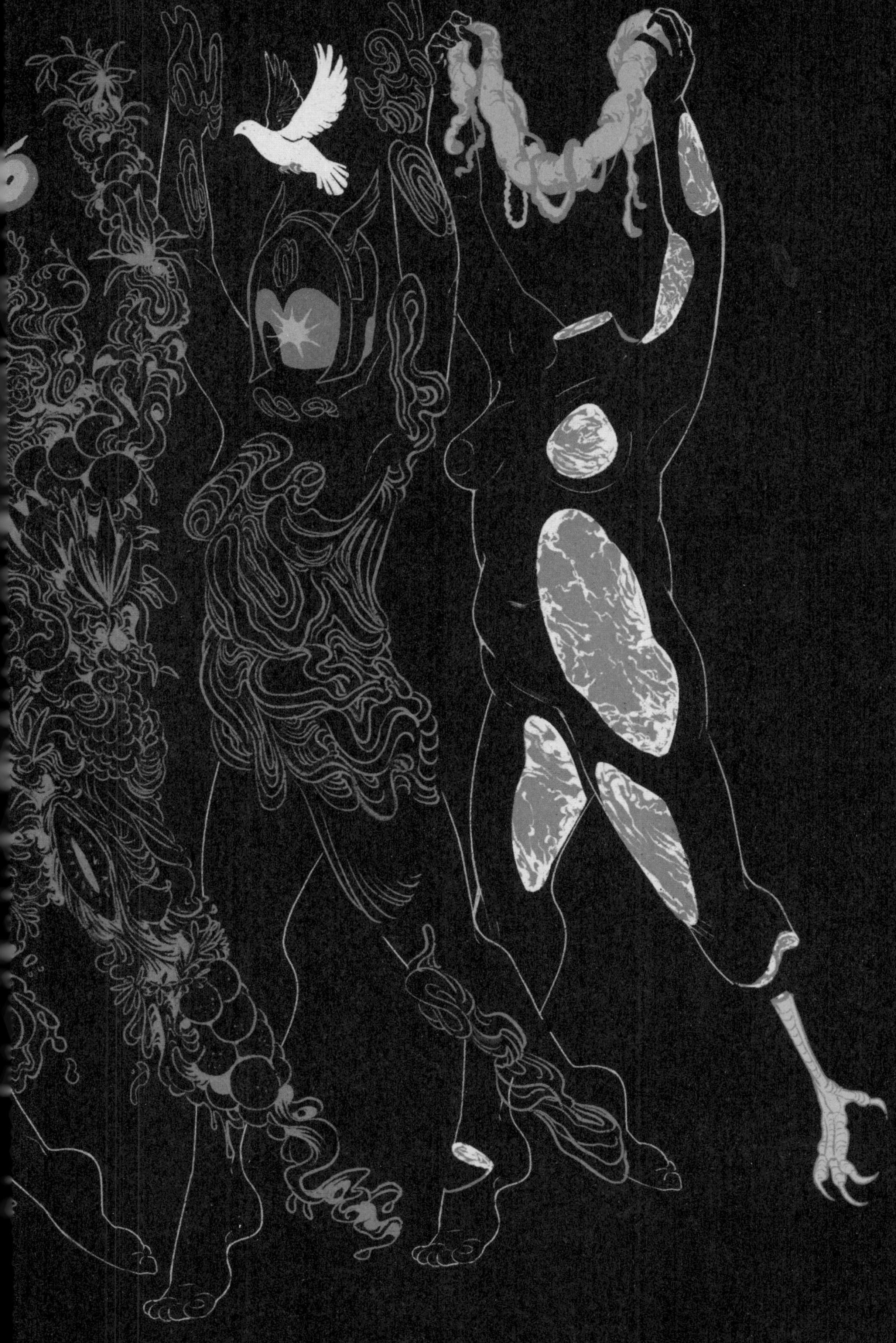

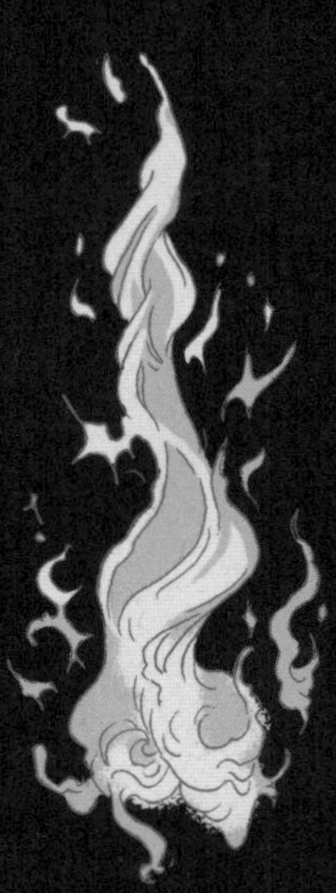

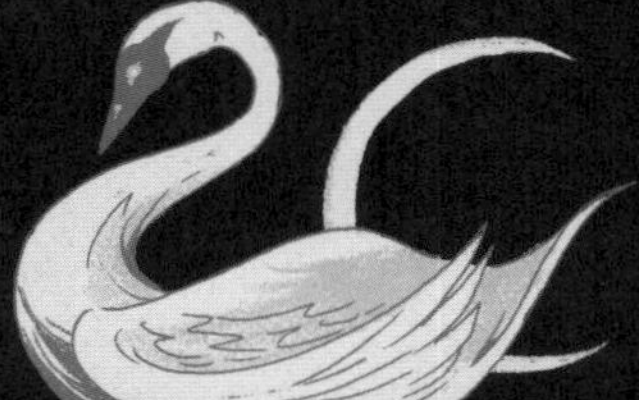

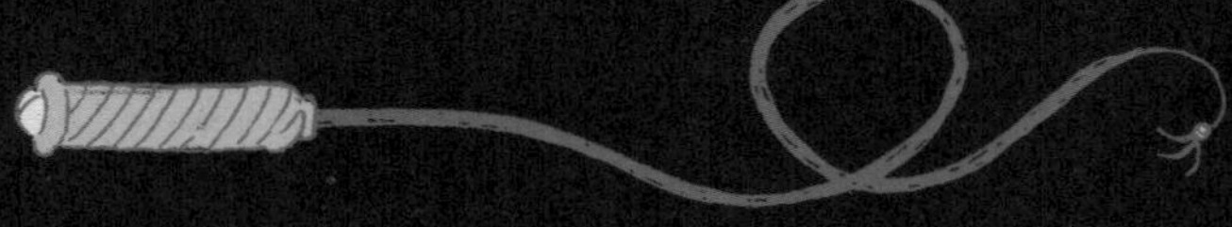

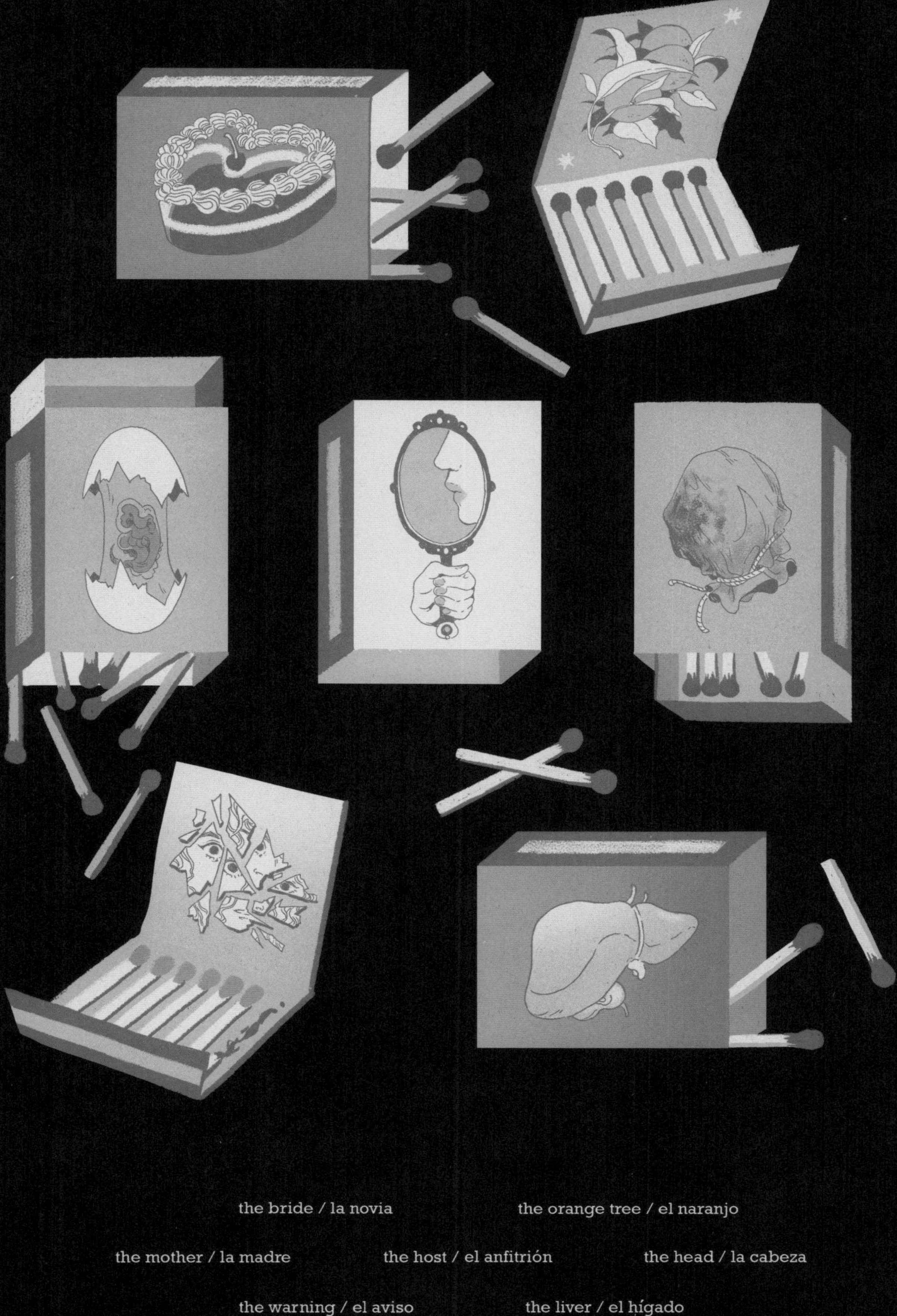

the bride / la novia

the orange tree / el naranjo

the mother / la madre

the host / el anfitrión

the head / la cabeza

the warning / el aviso

the liver / el hígado

what i will be waits for me out of the corner of my eye
beneath the snowmelt and the loam,
breathes out from my father's mouth, set like an
emerald beneath my mother's hair.

you, alchemist.
you, my salvation, given soft, irregular shape.
i will be ravenous again
when i can finally see your face.

lo que seré me espera por el rabillo del ojo
bajo el deshielo y la marga,
exhala de la boca de mi padre, engastada como una
esmeralda bajo el cabello de mi madre.

tú, alquimista.
tú, mi salvación, dada forma suave e irregular.
volveré a estar hambrienta
cuando finalmente pueda ver tu cara.

in the ruins, after the flood,
a pit will fall from my mouth where the snake feels the burn of its own bite
and a pearl will bloom in the blood of the cut.
grown from the grit of mourning,
drawn from the highest hitch of your laughter,
the deep echo of all that came before.
we'll make a picnic of the bitter rot clotting our hearts,
brush the sleep from each other's eyes.

let me never go hungry for you, let me grow heavy with your company.
when the weight lifts, all kisses turned to firsts, all touch divine,
when your jeweled breath dapples my skin under the same platinum sun,
in the wake, in heaven.

the summer, heavy-lidded,
arrives with arms stoned in dew
to teach me.
hyacinths jewel the charred pavement,
the city's pulse points doused
in beer and lilac.
with sweat-cooked bellies browning,
salt in my laugh lines,
it isn't hard to understand
that my use is to stand in awe,
witness to wonders that candy under my gaze,
adored,
to renew my vows to that hothouse flower
asleep in my chest.

there is no sea between us, no serpent below,
and if there's any part of me that can't remember
that to love you is to feel the hands of a god
pulling my hair back from my face
then the sun has bleached it from my sight.

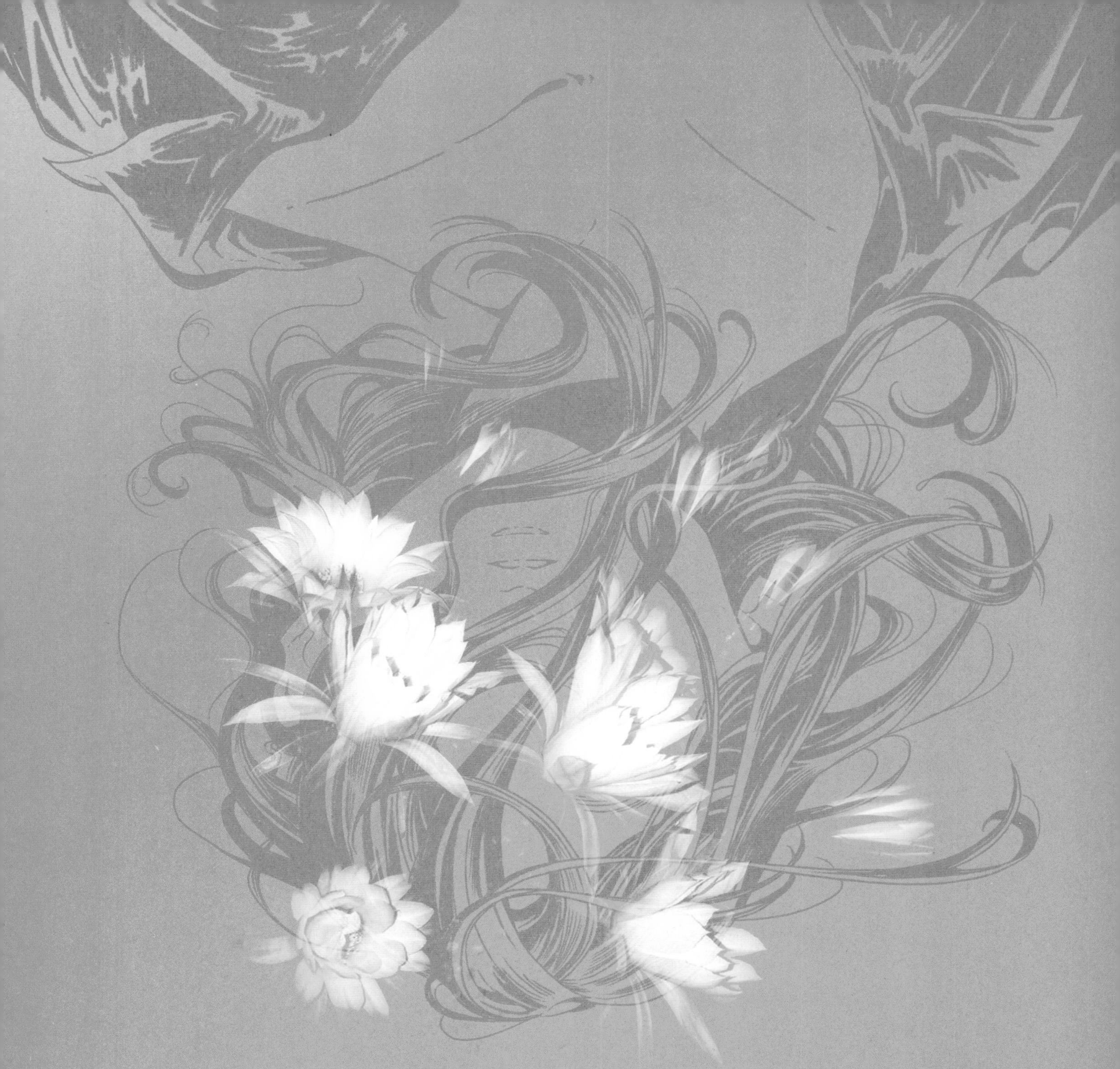

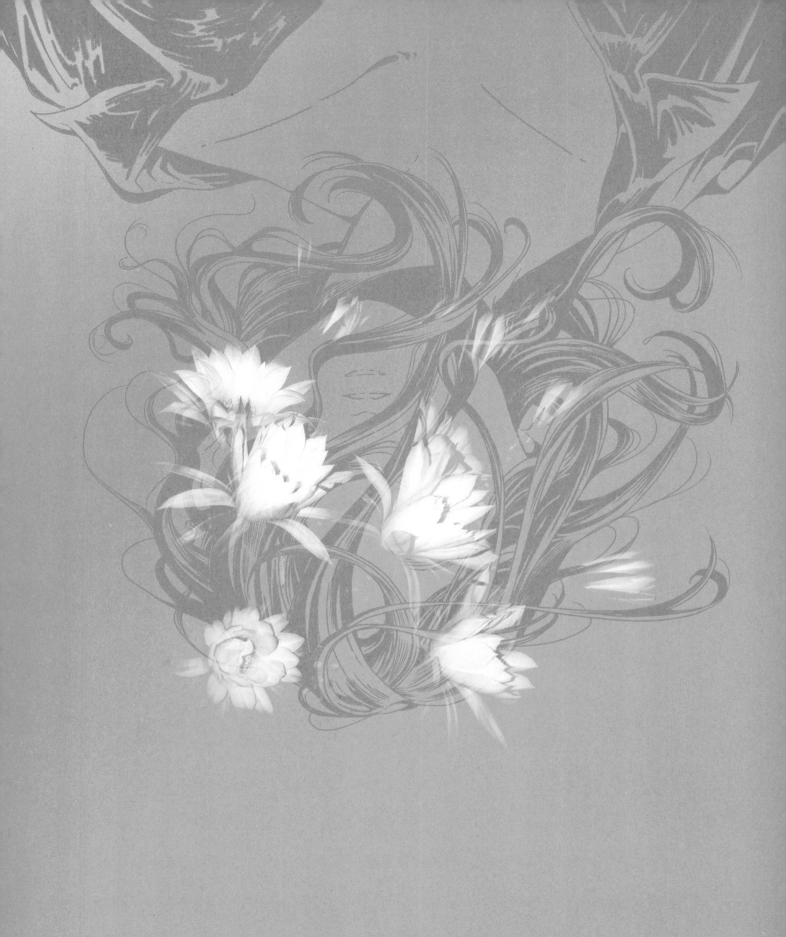

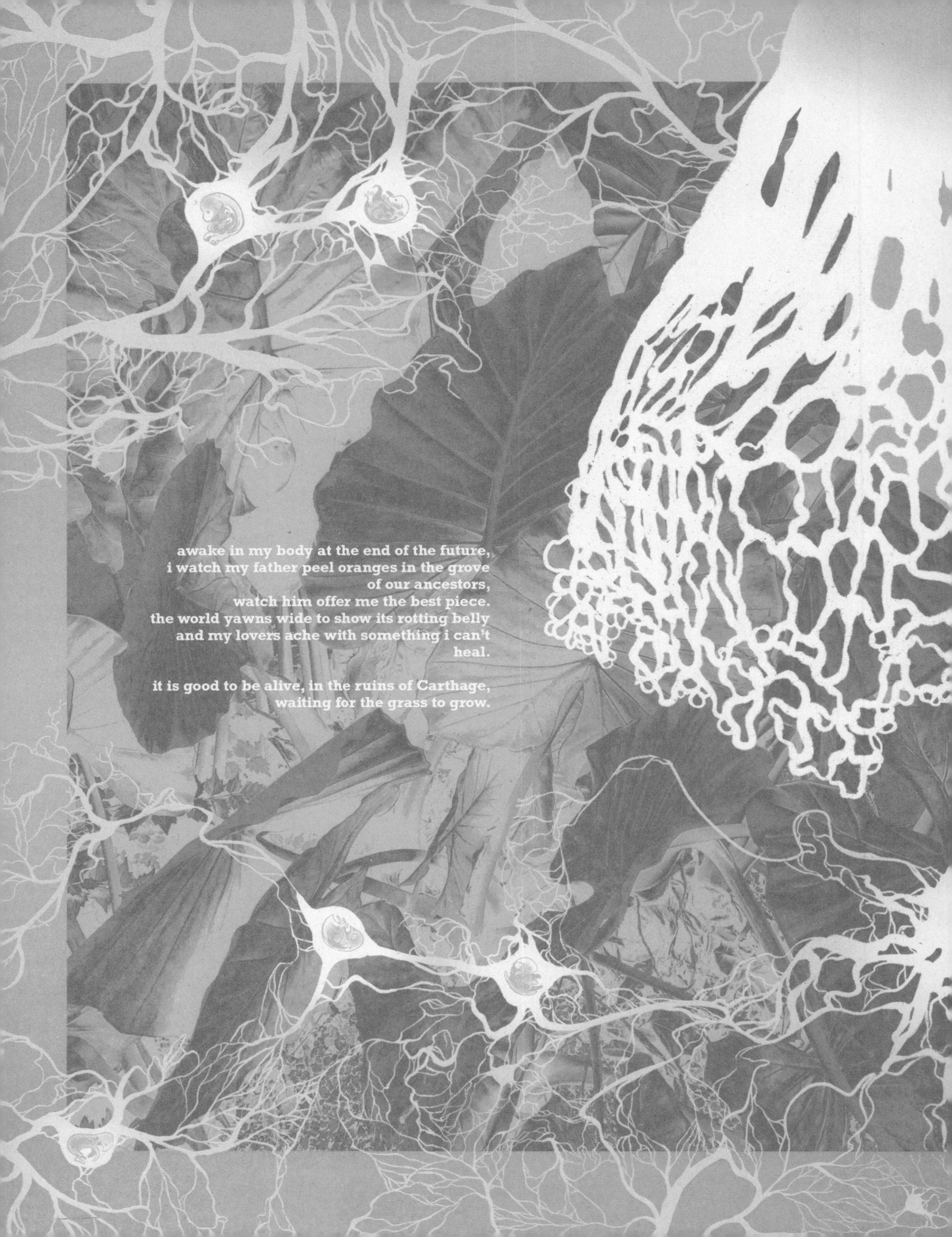

awake in my body at the end of the future,
i watch my father peel oranges in the grove
of our ancestors,
watch him offer me the best piece.
the world yawns wide to show its rotting belly
and my lovers ache with something i can't
heal.

it is good to be alive, in the ruins of Carthage,
waiting for the grass to grow.

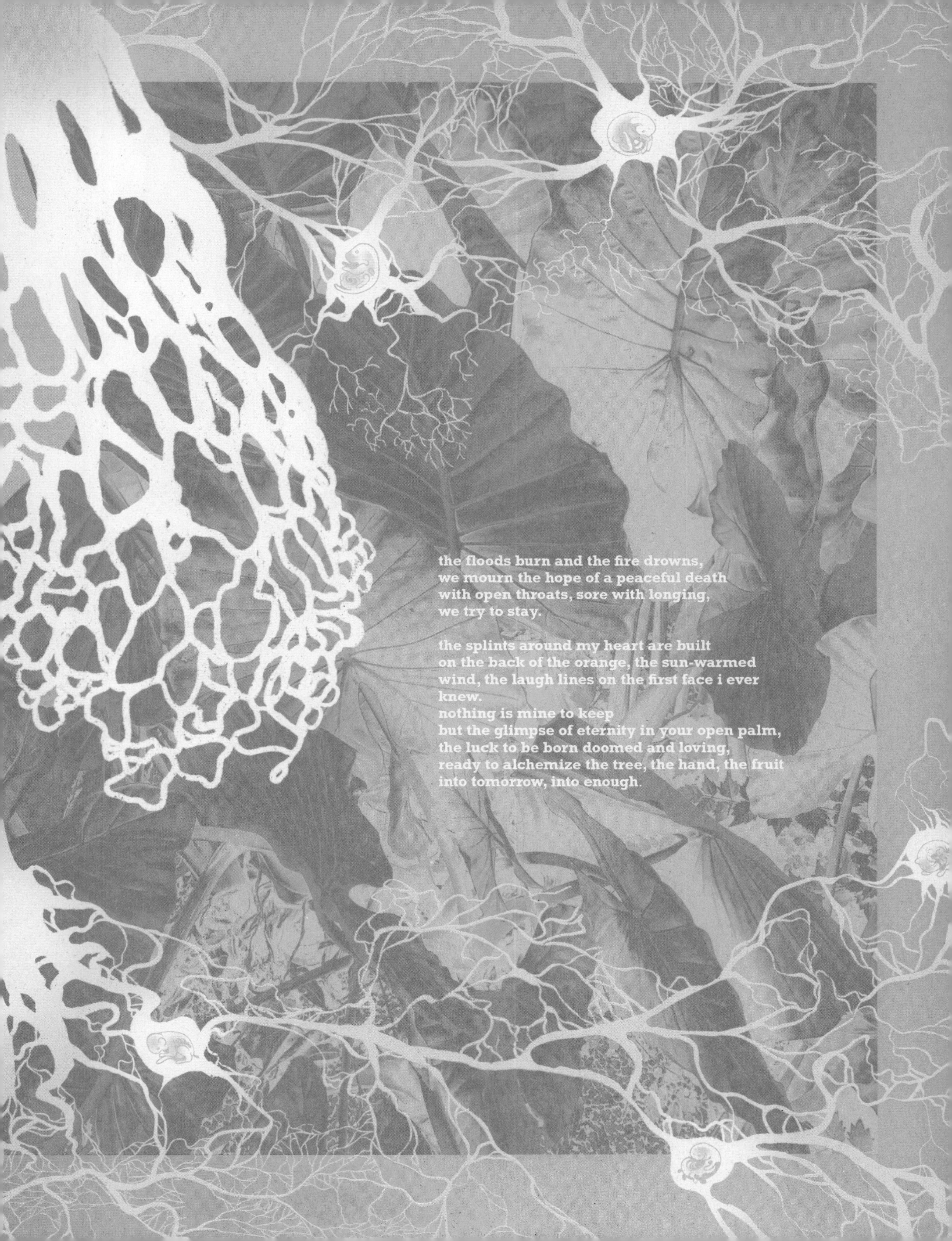

the floods burn and the fire drowns,
we mourn the hope of a peaceful death
with open throats, sore with longing,
we try to stay.

the splints around my heart are built
on the back of the orange, the sun-warmed
wind, the laugh lines on the first face i ever
knew.
nothing is mine to keep
but the glimpse of eternity in your open palm,
the luck to be born doomed and loving,
ready to alchemize the tree, the hand, the fruit
into tomorrow, into enough.

if i am a lemon
tree, still and
fragrant, i'll mark
your path with
heady spring 'til
you bring my
fruits inside, sit
serene in your
kitchen to watch
over your lover
while she cuts me
in two and serves
me chilled.

if i am a yak,
in my atelier of
yarn and mountain
flowers, i'll give
thick, clotted milk
to grow the bones
of infants, strong
enough to lean on.

if i am butter,
wet and animal
in chrysanthemum
yellow,
precious during
feast or famine,
then i will never
be purposeless on
your mantle,
an oil painting of
a hunting dog.
i will melt under a
hundred tongues
and still keep my
taste for yours.

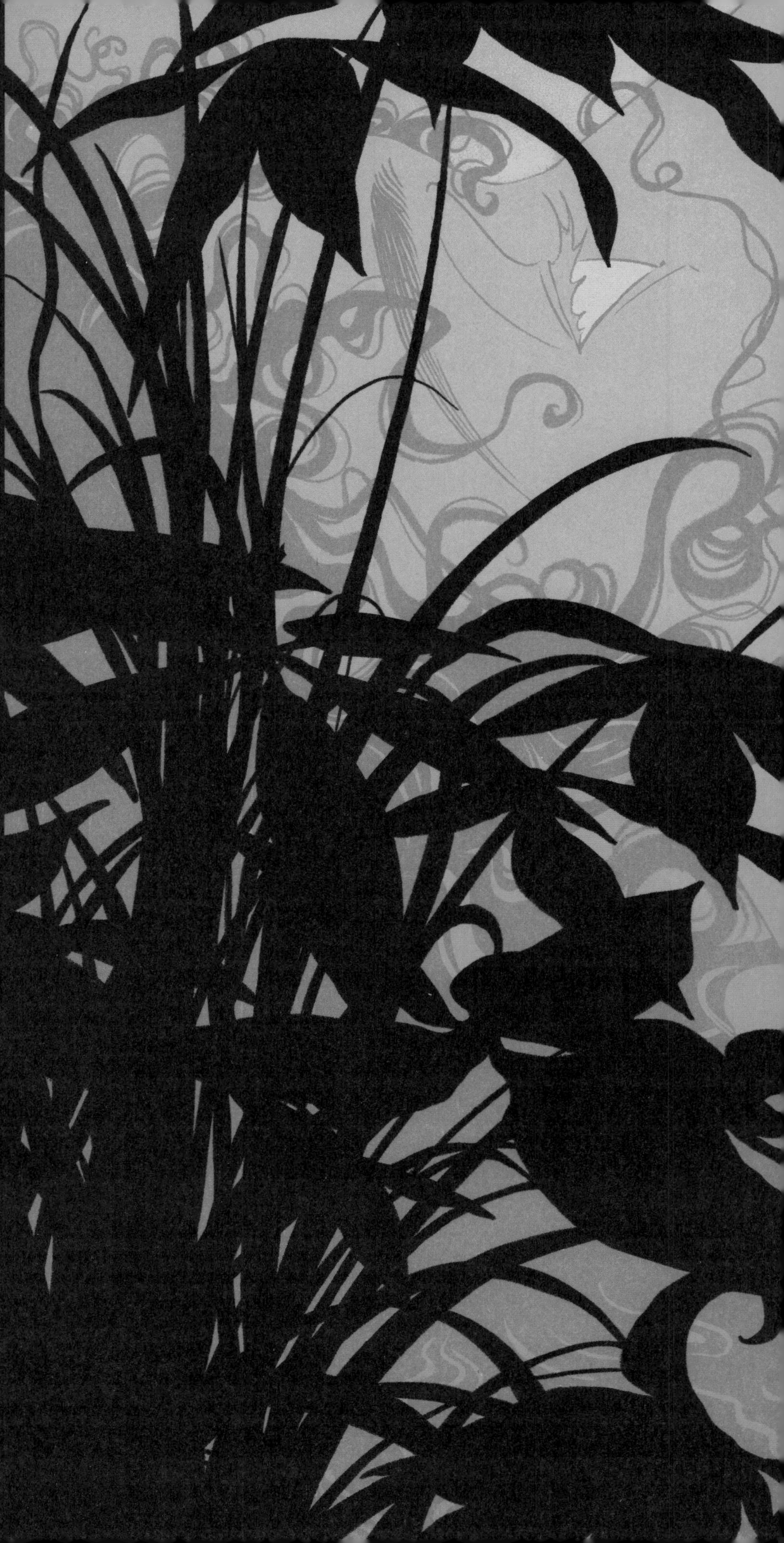

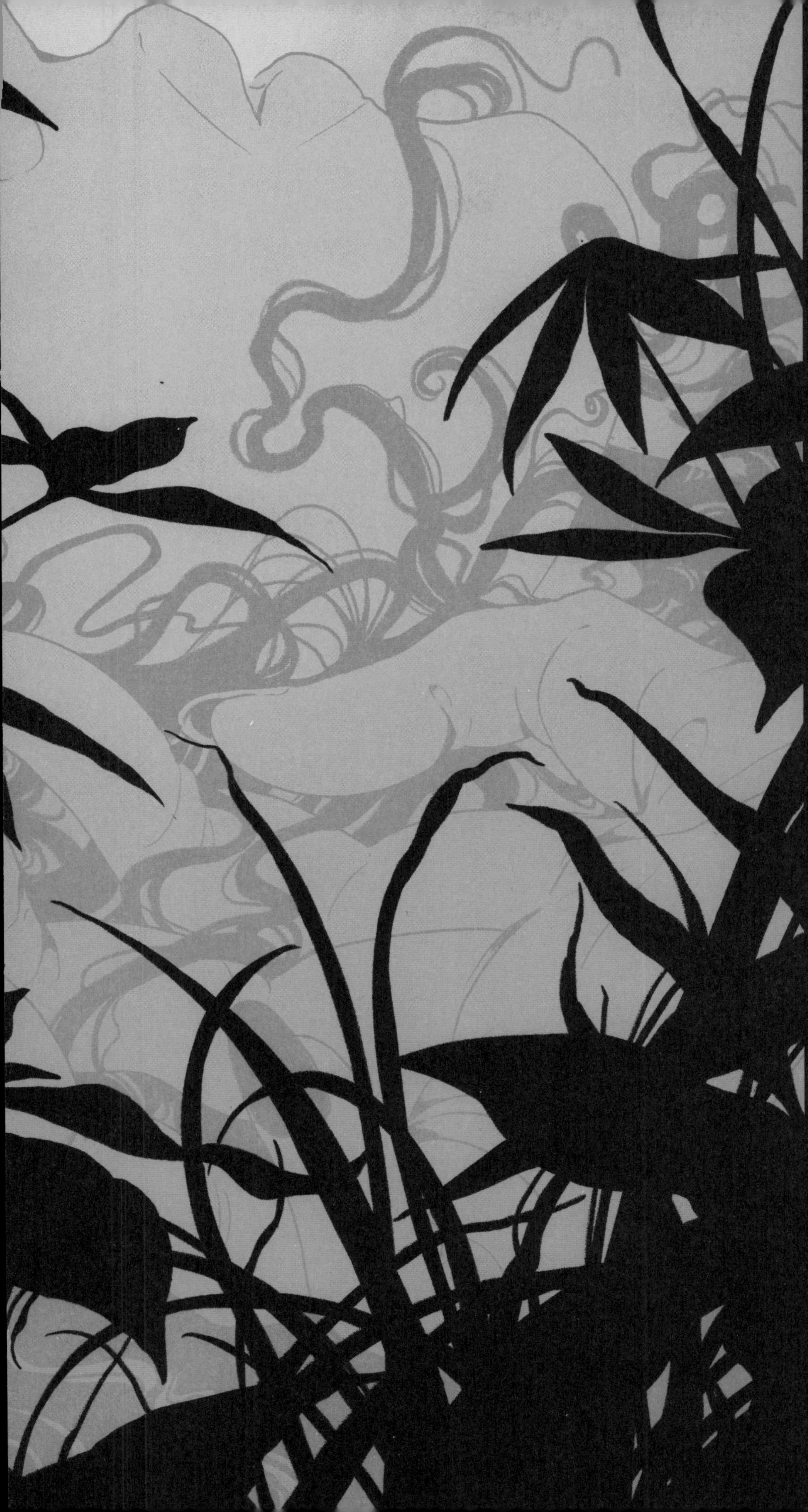

if i am the sea,
first cradle,
swollen with
pre-cambrian
ghosts, i'll be as
boundless as
you are definite,
the stained
glass of my
back turned to
the sun,
threaded with
poetry.

if i am moss,
mycelium,
white worm
grown from the
planet's heart,
tapestry of all
mother tongues,
i'll translate
dogwood to
baobab, stitch
the dead back
into the living,
sew all hearts to
mine.

if you love me,
then i am loved.
if you love me,
then i am loved.
if you love me,
then i am loved.

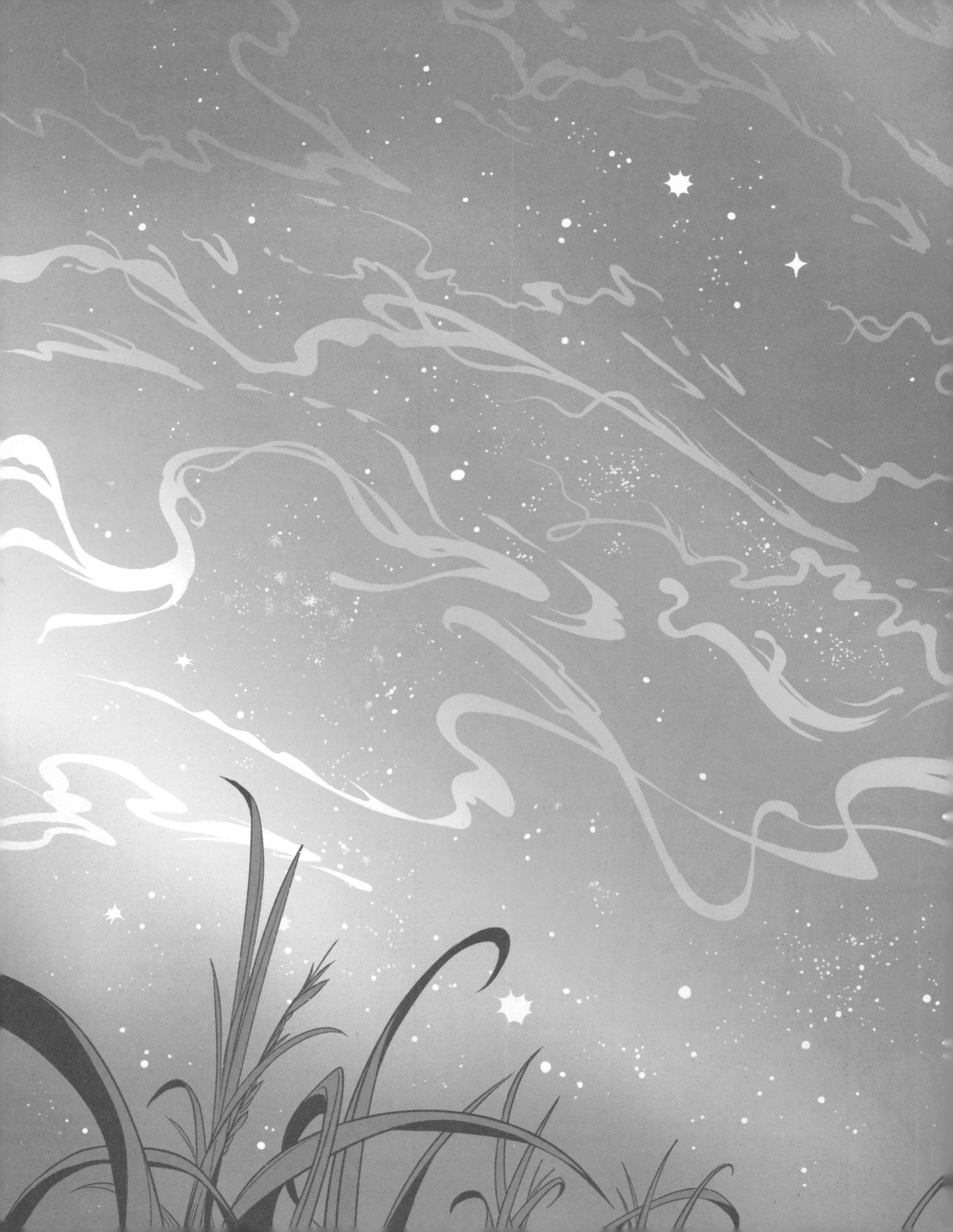

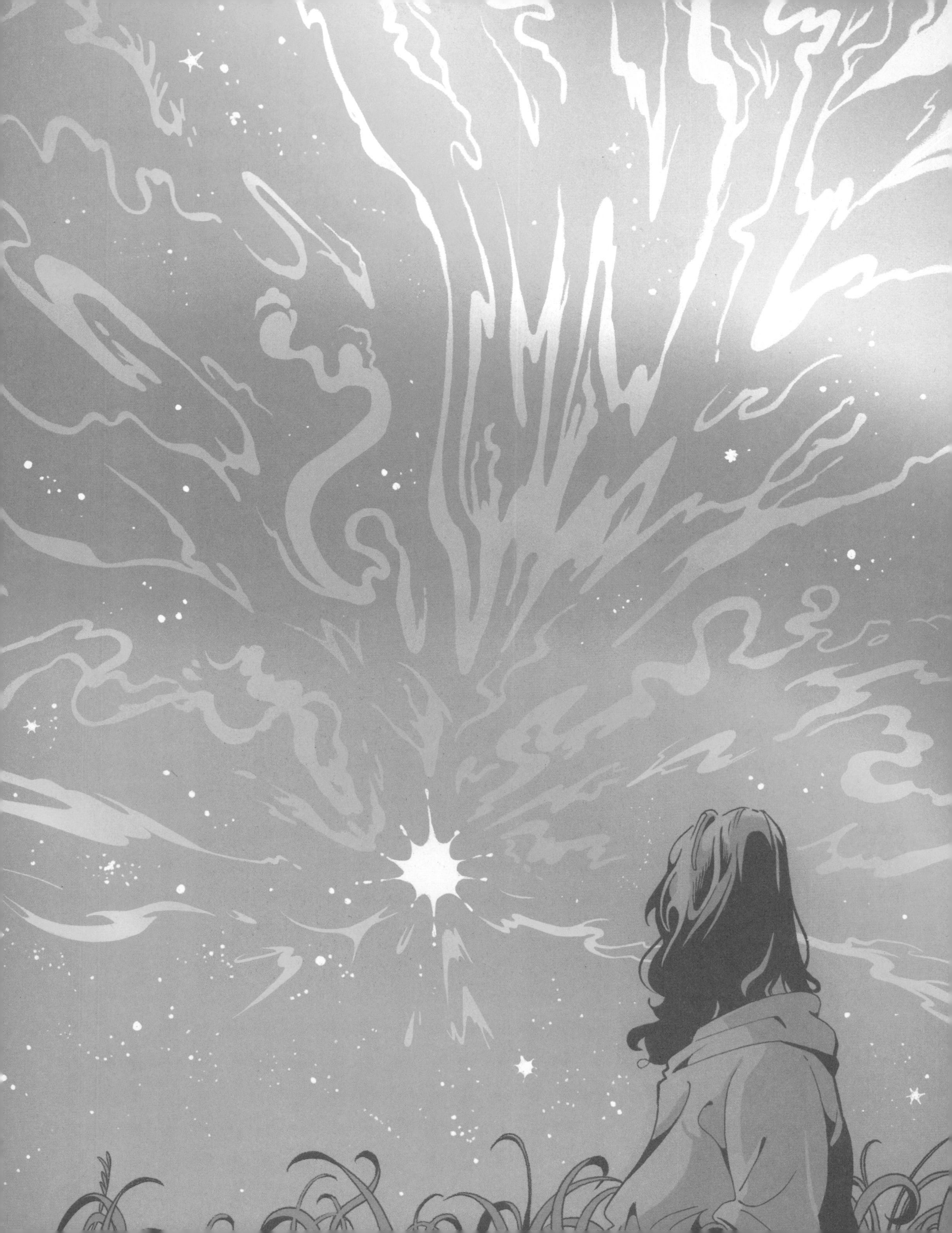

Written and illustrated by Rosemary Valero-O'Connell
hirosemary.com / @hirosemaryhello

ISBN 979-8-88620-000-3
First Printing, February 2023
Printed in China

Published by:
Silver Sprocket
1018 Valencia St, San Francisco, CA 94110, USA
www.silversprocket.net

Avi Ehrlich, Publisher
Josh PM, General Manager
Ari Yarwood, Managing Editor
Carina Taylor, Production Designer
Daniel Zhou, Shop Rat
Raul Higuera-Cortez, Big Head Bandit
Sarah Maloney, Shop Cat
Sol Cintron, Fruit Bat
Tori Bowler, Shop Cryptid